Corporate Sustainability in India

A Practical Guide for Multinationals

Caroline Twigg

caroline.twigg1@gmail.com

www.linkedin.com/pub/caroline-twigg/0/214/909

First published in 2013 by Dō Sustainability

87 Lonsdale Road, Oxford OX2 7ET, UK

ISBN 978-1-909293-76-2 (eBook-ePub)
ISBN 978-1-909293-77-9 (eBook-PDF)
ISBN 978-1-909293-75-5 (Paperback)

A catalogue record for this title is available from the British Library.

Dō Sustainability strives for net positive social and environmental impact. See our sustainability policy at **www.dosustainability.com**.

Page design and typesetting by Alison Rayner
Cover by Becky Chilcott

For further information on Dō Sustainability, visit our website: **www.dosustainability.com**

DōShorts

Dō Sustainability is the publisher of DōShorts: short, high-value ebooks that distil sustainability best practice and business insights for busy, results-driven professionals. Each DōShort can be read in 90 minutes.

New and forthcoming DōShorts – stay up to date

We publish 3 to 5 new DōShorts each month. The best way to keep up to date? Sign up to our short, monthly newsletter. Go to **www.dosustainability.com/newsletter** to sign up to the Dō Newsletter. Some of our latest and forthcoming titles include:

- *How to Engage Youth to Drive Corporate Responsbility: Roles and Interventions*   Nicolò Wojewoda
- *The Short Guide to Sustainable Investing*   Cary Krosinsky
- *Strategic Sustainability: Why it Matters to Your Business and How to Make it Happen*   Alexandra McKay
- *Sustainability Decoded: How to Unlock Profit Through the Value Chain*   Laura Musikanski
- *Working Collaboratively: A Practical Guide to Achieving More*   Penny Walker
- *Understanding G4: The Concise Guide to Next Generation Sustainability Reporting*   Elaine Cohen
- *Leading Sustainable Innovation*   Nick Coad & Paul Pritchard
- *Leadership for Sustainability and Change*   Cynthia Scott & Tammy Esteves
- *The Social Licence to Operate: Your Management Framework for Complex Times*   Leeora Black

- *Building a Sustainable Supply Chain*   Gareth Kane
- *Management Systems for Sustainability: How to Successfully Connect Strategy and Action*   Phil Cumming
- *Understanding Integrated Reporting: The Concise Guide to Integrated Thinking and the Future of Corporate Reporting*
  Carol Adams

Subscriptions

In addition to individual sales of our ebooks, we now offer subscriptions. Access 60+ ebooks for the price of 5 with a personal subscription to our full e-library. Institutional subscriptions are also available for your staff or students. Visit **www.dosustainability.com/books/subscriptions** or email **veruschka@dosustainability.com**

Write for us, or suggest a DōShort

Please visit **www.dosustainability.com** for our full publishing programme. If you don't find what you need, write for us! Or suggest a DōShort on our website. We look forward to hearing from you.

....

Abstract

THIS DŌ SHORT HELPS international companies outside of India to understand their potential engagement around sustainability issues there, and offers practical insights into making this successful. It is relevant to professionals in varied roles whether they are hoping to expand their business and have products or services with a sustainability focus, or they sit in a communications team in a corporate HQ tasked with explaining their operations' sustainability work in India, or are running a foundation with projects in India. It offers insight into doing business in India in general; the history and culture of the country which has shaped business engagement with society and the environment over time; how companies already work on sustainability issues and what might come in the future. The Short also includes helpful immediate steps and action for people wanting to take their involvement in the country further. It is a first step to help foreigners understand the corporate sustainability field in India, and engage with it respectfully, effectively and easily.

About the Author

 **CAROLINE TWIGG** is an international sustainability professional who has lived and worked in Delhi, Geneva and London. She set up the India office of the World Business Council for Sustainable Development (WBCSD), helping to establish programmes on low-carbon technology and safety with the Indian cement industry, to develop a water risk assessment tool for companies operating in India, to bring together industry and government around urban infrastructure planning, to devise business and ecosystems training for companies, and to build engagement around sustainability among Indian industries. Before India, Caroline worked at WBCSD and at the International Union for the Conservation of Nature (IUCN) in Geneva, and at Good Business consultancy in London.

She is particularly interested in partnership and collaboration, the changing role of business in sustainability, business growth that can support emerging economy development, urban infrastructure and city development, and how business can bring solutions to the challenges of today and tomorrow.

Caroline studied geography at Oxford University, has an MProf in Leadership for Sustainable Development from Forum for the Future and Middlesex University, and a Post Graduate Certificate in Cross-sector

ABOUT THE AUTHOR

Partnerships from Cambridge University. She is happily married to a husband who shares her love of adventure and travel, and they can often be seen playing tennis, hiking in the hills, cycling, camping, or paddling their canoe on the Thames.

....

Acknowledgements

I'M GRATEFUL TO MY WONDERFUL peer reviewers, friends and family: Sarah Holloway, Sachin Joshi, Stephen Redrup and Martin Wright. Your feedback and insight has made this much more interesting, readable and relevant. And I'm grateful to Mother India and her people, for inviting me in, chewing me up, wearing me down and then getting me excited all over again, and finally spitting me out wondering if anything I've learnt will still be relevant in 10 years time.

Contents

CHAPTER 1
What's This All About?

AFTER SOME YEARS based in Geneva at the headquarters of the World Business Council for Sustainable Development (WBCSD), I had the incredible opportunity to be their 'presence on the ground' in India. Eventually setting up a physical office, hiring staff and formally incorporating the organisation there, my three-year adventure in the world of business and sustainability in India has shaped much of my thought on how business engages with and drives sustainability in the country.

My journey took me to a cement plant in rural Chhattisgarh to discuss road safety with 20 truck company owners and 40 illiterate drivers; to a city in Gujarat that saw a quarter of its population flee during a plague outbreak in 1994; to a private lounge 20 floors up in a Delhi five-star hotel discussing urban infrastructure with a former Minister, and to the shiny glass offices of Mumbai to convince Indian conglomerates with annual revenues of over $70 bn they should send their staff on business and biodiversity training. A day in India is always unique.

You cannot be in India without feeling the urgency of sustainability challenges. Some countries feel they have the liberty to discuss and debate, but in India everything is changing by the hour – the country and its people won't wait for international agreements on climate change or long processes they don't see the value in. However, many of the solutions actually underway are too short-termist, too ad hoc, too inefficient.

Industry has an unquestionable role in the growth of any nation, and in India it is increasingly working to help ensure that developmental goals are achieved alongside growth.

So many (wonderful) books on India are hundreds of pages long. This publication is not one of those. Focusing on its huge variety and complexity, it's not easy to distil so much into 100 pages. That means it's *not* a scientifically rigorous, practitioner-tested compendium of 'doing sustainability' in India. It is an insight, based on experience, as to how the international concept of sustainability features in the meeting rooms of India's businesses, and how that impacts communities and natural landscapes. It is supposed to help a 'ferengi'/'eengleeshman'/'amreekan' understand what's driving sustainability in India. And what's not. It's aimed at company representatives from elsewhere who are looking to do business in India in 'a sustainable way', or to promote sustainable development in the Indian business world for whatever reason they may have. I imagine that Indian nationals would reject some of these words as incorrect as understood from within. But most outsiders trying to operate in the Indian context see things differently from nationals themselves, and a 'translation service' to help bridge that divide is a helpful addition to the toolbox for foreigners with a Jet Airways ticket in their bag. I'm an outsider with an insight and that's what I'm trying to bring here.

Because of my office location, my lens is mostly on Delhi: the elitist, showy, urgently aspirational capital city where rich heirs aim to own a black SUV, and where who-you-know-and-how-you-can-demonstrate-that is a symbol of how important you are. This doesn't help to explain the characteristics of the many other areas of India.

I now live in London and I left India with mixed emotions. I feel hopeful.

I'm encouraged by the energy that any project can generate with the right people behind it and in spite of restrictive, opaque and seemingly endless processes. I'm encouraged by the increasing pressure on all parts of society to consult widely and use the democratic system effectively, to ensure any company's social licence to operate is offered by a willing community within a natural environment that can support those operations. I feel overwhelmed. I'm continually amazed at the scale of the challenges, the interwoven complexities which are further muddled by the chaotic manner of development and the urgency in which all things happen. And I feel humbled. And respectful of the many people who battle all odds to promote a partnership approach to good water management in one river basin, who innovate to map slum alleys by GPS so deliveries can be made even where street addresses don't exist, and the young people who push against a tradition of rote-learning to take initiative and find solutions for problems the outside world doesn't see. Quickly in London I recognised my former life here. So much is different, yet so little has changed. I cannot see the same happening if I return to India in 2020. I hope this guide is useful for people from elsewhere who have a sustainability ambition for their work in India.

....

CHAPTER 2

What You Need to Know About India

"India has never been a country; it has always been a dream, an idea, an elusive vision." GITANJALI KOLANAD

A land of contrasts

WHILE LIVING IN ONE PART OF INDIA, it's common to be asked for an opinion on a recent news story in another part of the country – what do you think of the way the water is managed in Rajasthan? What about Public Private Partnerships for urban infrastructure being set up in Gujarat? Although many people will have *some* understanding, they won't know all the detail. It can feel like being Swedish and being asked your views on wastewater treatment in Greece – unless you're an expert in exactly that, you really can't speculate without having been. Just because you're based in one part of India it doesn't mean you know much about the whole country. India is a sub-continent in itself, a huge and varied landmass of sprawling subsistence farms interspersed with pulsating metropolises that expand daily, outwards with immigrants and upwards with new buildings. Different religions dominate in different regions and shape the way of living lives and doing business. Languages, dress, gender equality, climate, landscape lifestyle, infrastructure – all vary enormously from place to place. In contrast to most foreigners' perception, India is most definitely not one homogenous country. Some say what unites the 1.2 billion Indians is being part of the 'largest democracy in the world', a fact Indians are hugely proud of (714 million Indians registered to vote in the last elections). But in all other aspects of life, the variety is huge.

> *Sustainability issues are varied and widespread – understanding one issue in one area doesn't necessarily mean you can apply that knowledge across India.*

Natural resources

India is a 'mega-diverse' country with 2.4% of the world's land mass, but 7–8% of global species including a huge 91,000 species of animals and 45,500 species of plants. India is home to about half the world's wild tigers, as well as keystone species such as the leopard, elephant, one-horned rhino and Ganges river dolphin.

Many natural areas are being damaged or exploited as populations grow: animals' habitats are pressured – for example, leopards are increasingly killing village livestock or inhabitants – and industrial growth is leading to land use change – for example, converting elephants' natural fodder (200 kg a day per elephant) into lakes for hydro-electric power or plantations for timber. Environmental permission processes are often controversial and the Ministry of Environment and Forests creaks under the pressure of sanctioning multiple land use requests across the country. India mines 89 minerals including iron ore, bauxite and coal (its major fuel source). Awareness and valuation of ecosystems services is much lower in India than in developed countries – an understanding of the long-term impact of industrial growth on ecosystems is poor, and very few companies assess their dependencies on ecosystems and their services. As land use pressure continues to grow, the importance of this issue will increase in the future.

Access to water (both the provision of *enough* water and access to *clean and safe* water) is a highly controversial and problematic challenge for Indian business, communities, farmers and governments at all levels. As in any country, industrial operations require water to run machinery and equipment, to use in products and packaging, and for employees. Industry also often discharges water from its operations and must ensure any water leaving its sites is unpolluted. In India, the industrial sector uses about 6% of all available water (about 92% is used for irrigation). There is a growing understanding that companies that manage water poorly will be exposed to increased costs and operational risks; reputational and regulatory risks; risks to the health of employees; risks to markets and products; and financial risks, for example, from investors. Many individual companies are working on their own water efficiency and good water management processes, and several collaborative efforts are underway by organisations like Colombia University's Water Centre, FICCI and WBCSD. However, poor quality data, low maintenance of water infrastructure, erratic monsoons, illegal water use and so on, exacerbate the issue.

Access to natural resources, including water, is a continual challenge for India's poor. Indian industry can often find itself in lengthy processes to obtain permission for access, yet collaborative approaches, e.g. on watershed management, are increasingly being tried.

Development

Statistics about poverty in India can often be hard to take in because the numbers are so large: 828 million people live on less than $2 a day; 400 million people don't have electricity; more people have access to a mobile phone than a toilet; 46% of global maternal deaths are in India; there are more people living in the eight poorest states than in the 26 poorest countries of Africa combined and so on – the huge figures can often overwhelm people, and the actual ground reality of the numbers can be lost. However, the scale of the challenge should never be underestimated.

The ambition to see India 'develop' is central to all government policy and approaches, and is the focus of much study and research, as well as business action. Everyone agrees development is vital to bring millions of people out of poverty and to ensure India is a key player in the global economy. (The question, and often inertia, is just around how that can happen.) Gender inequality is stark in India: the country ranks only 136 out of 186 countries on UNDP's Gender Inequality Index which includes indicators of empowerment, workplace participation and reproductive health. However, it's also the case that some private sector companies have highly respected female senior leaders, particularly in the finance or service industries.

The potential trade-off between development and environment is much more apparent than in developed countries. A growing population and industrial presence will only increase this. Business has long felt a responsibility towards 'nation-building' and all CSR/sustainability approaches must be framed in the context of poverty alleviation to be really supported and successful.

Government and leadership

India currently has a coalition government, led by the Indian National Congress. The main opposition party is the Bharatiya Janata Party (BJP). Each state democratically votes in the leadership of its own region. The Communist government ruled in some of the largest states until 2012. General elections must take place at least every five years and the next will be in 2014. Parliament consists of two houses: directly elected 552-member Lok Sabha (House of the People), and the 245-member indirectly elected Rajya Sabha (Council of the States), following from the British system. The Prime Minister and Council of Ministers are responsible to the Lok Sabha. The President is Head of State and has mostly ceremonial duties.

In recent years Parliament has stalled for whole sessions (two to three months), log-jamming new policy and reforms, and there is increasing criticism of ineffectual leadership by aged politicians. It's often said by business people in India that business is successful 'in spite of the government' not because of it and its policies. A wider trend is the emergence of regional parties and politicians, who, in India's federal structure, often wield considerable power.

> *Every state decides its own duties, taxes and import/export rules, so you should consider how easily you can move your goods or source your raw materials in the area in which you wish to operate in India. States, by Constitution, have more power than the central administration in Delhi, and this is increasingly being seen in practice.*

Economic growth and uncertainty

The Government of India focuses huge efforts on promoting continued economic growth believing this to be the route to prosperity for all. The 2012–13 rate of 5% which 'might be considered a crawl in India, is still among the world's fastest' (Hindustan Times, 6 July 2013). India's position as a service centre, the world's back office, is well-known. However, there has never been an industrial revolution or widespread industrial growth in the country, and subsequently there is very little manufacturing expertise and capacity. The Economist published a lucid article in mid-2013 outlining how thousands of unskilled young men are seeking work (either in rural areas or having recently arrived in urban areas), yet only able to take on roles as, for example, security guards outside shops or cash points, or as migrant labour.[1] For them, a lack of vocational training means no obvious future opportunities and no clear progression to positions of higher responsibility. The ability of the country's unskilled or semi-skilled young people to find work in the future will depend on access to vocational training. In addition, anti-corruption protests and demonstrations about violence against women in 2012–2013 showed widespread discontent among the educated urban youth. The public's acceptance of corruption in government in particular, but in business and all areas of life in general, will be less and less.

Economic growth is a key focus of all politicians. There is an important opportunity for Indian and international business to demonstrate that embedding sustainability within business can support India's long-term growth.

Energy and power

Electricity infrastructure in India is very unreliable, and an estimated 27% of electricity is tapped off the grid illegally or lost in transmission before reaching its destination. Farmers are not required to pay for electricity to pump water and irrigate their fields, leading to huge wastage and inefficiencies. The 2012 blackouts affecting 620 million people were well documented globally. With the potential of such blackouts in mind, industry has spent nearly $30 billion building independent power provision (for example, captive power plants alongside cement kilns), to ensure a reliable supply of power to their factories. Fifty-seven percent of electricity is powered by coal (much imported as India's is of low quality), 19% by hydropower, 12% by other renewable sources (solar power is increasing but the investment costs are high, and there is very little opportunity for wind power in most of the country), natural gas accounts for 9%, and nuclear about 2%. Biomass remains a key energy source for the poor.

> *Energy infrastructure is unreliable for business operations. A huge number of people live without access to energy – this presents a large opportunity for the provision of access to energy, e.g. micro-generation by business.*

Infrastructure and connectivity

Many Indians quote the top four things they are happy to have inherited from British rule: democracy, the English language, cricket and the railways. Indian Railways is said to be the second largest employer in the world, and 115,000 km of track winds through the over-crowded cities and off into the least accessible and least inhabited areas of the country. Twenty-five million passengers and 2.8 million tons of freight are transported daily. Tickets are cheap and virtually everyone in India can afford to travel because of the railway. However, the network is creaking with over-use, and ticket prices are rising. Alongside this, investment in other infrastructure has been woeful and is only well thought-through and joined up in a few cases: India has just 4 km of paved and unpaved roads per 1000 people (USA has 21 km), and the McKinsey Global Institute estimates that India needs to build 800 m^2 of floor space and 400 km of railway track every year until 2030 to be able to adequately house and move its populations and businesses. The road network carries over 65% of freight and contributes about 5% to GDP (rail transport about 1%). However, around 40% of fresh goods are estimated to go off on the way to market. Domestic air travel is growing rapidly.

If India's physical connectivity is a bad news story, India's mobile connectivity is a great news day. This has leapfrogged grid connectivity and driven much business and development in all corners of the country. Businesses are run on mobile phones, market pricing information is circulated and money moved between relatives around the world, phones with multiple address books enable shared use by several people, text messages remind new mothers living in slums (i.e. without an address) to take their babies for vaccinations on the right day. India has one of the lowest call tariffs in the world enabled by huge telephone networks and strong competition, and the uptake continues to grow. The 150 million internet users represent only a 12% penetration rate, yet more than half the phones bought in 2010 were smartphones. According to a Nokia Siemens Networks study, mobile data in India grew 92% year-on-year in the 2012/13 financial year; at one point, Vodafone attracted two million new customers a month.

India's physical infrastructure makes logistics and 'last mile' sustainability projects challenging, but continued rapid growth and innovation in mobile connectivity provides an opportunity to bring information, data and knowledge to many of India's poor or rural communities.

Map of India with key business centres

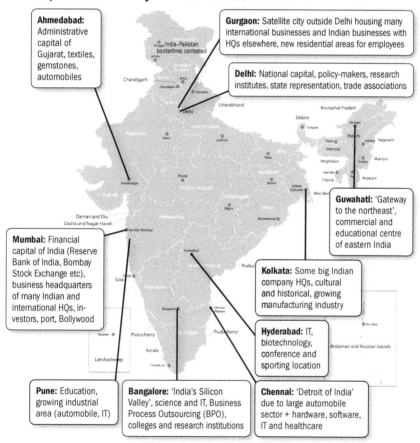

Ahmedabad: Administrative capital of Gujarat, textiles, gemstones, automobiles

Gurgaon: Satellite city outside Delhi housing many international businesses and Indian businesses with HQs elsewhere, new residential areas for employees

Delhi: National capital, policy-makers, research institutes, state representation, trade associations

Guwahati: 'Gateway to the northeast', commercial and educational centre of eastern India

Mumbai: Financial capital of India (Reserve Bank of India, Bombay Stock Exchange etc), business headquarters of many Indian and international HQs, investors, port, Bollywood

Kolkata: Some big Indian company HQs, cultural and historical, growing manufacturing industry

Hyderabad: IT, biotechnology, conference and sporting location

Pune: Education, growing industrial area (automobile, IT)

Bangalore: 'India's Silicon Valley', science and IT, Business Process Outsourcing (BPO), colleges and research institutions

Chennai: 'Detroit of India' due to large automobile sector + hardware, software, IT and healthcare

Quick statistics

TABLE 1. Quick statistics

Populous?	Populous: 1.22 billion (2013 estimate) (17.5% of the world's population)
Young or old?	Young: >50% of population under 25
Long life or short?	Increasing from 67.5 (men), 72.6 (women) (2009 estimates)
Rural or urban?	Rural for now (72% live in villages and 28% in town or cities), but increasingly urban (UN State of the World Population report 2012 estimates 40.76% urban by 2030)
Diverse or homogenous?	Diverse: 35 states and territories, > 2,000 ethnic groups, all major religions, 216 languages, huge variation in social parameters, e.g. income and education levels
Rich or poor?	Both: 55 billionaires (2013); 68.7% of population live on <$2 a day (World Bank 2010)
Literate or illiterate?	74% literacy rate (82% for men, 65% for women) (2011 census)
Many large cities?	13 cities with populations over 2 million. Mumbai: 12.48 million, Delhi 11 million, Bangalore 8.43 million, Hyderabad 6.80 million, Ahmedabad 5.57 million

Top business schools?	Indian Institutes of Management (IIMs) (in Ahmedabad, Kolkata, Bangalore, Indore, Kozhikode), Faculty of Management Studies Delhi, NMIMS, MDI Gurgaon, SP Jain Institute of Management and Resources Mumbai, XLRI School of Business and Human Resources Jamshedpur
Easy to do business?	Not really: ranked 132nd globally in the World Bank's 2013 Ease of Doing Business report

CHAPTER 3

What You Should Know About Doing Business in India

" No big international company can do without an India strategy. **"**
THE ECONOMIST

Everyone wants to do business in India

SINCE ECONOMIC LIBERALISATION IN 1991, the Indian economy has been increasingly open, and continues to attract interest from around the world. Global governments continue to court India: US President Obama and UK Prime Minister Cameron have both taken their largest foreign visit delegations to India, Chinese Premier Li Keqiang visited in May 2013 and the Brazilian President in August 2013, and many countries are vying to be India's 'partner of choice' for trade, education and bi-lateral relations, etc. And the international business world looks to India as a pool of cheap labour, IT services, and potentially the biggest new consumer base globally. Multi-national companies continue to demonstrate their long-term ambitions for growth in India: for example, Unilever CEO Paul Polman described its Indian partner as 'an excellent Indian business with . . . the potential for attractive long-term growth' as the UK-based company acquired an additional 14.8% stake in Hindustan Unilever Ltd in July 2013. Bilateral trade between India and China is worth $75.6 billion and is expected to reach $100 billion by 2015.

The country's many Non-Resident Indians ('NRIs') around the world have long facilitated these relationships. The rise of senior executives of Indian origin in global corporations is well-documented, but two new trends are now being seen as well:

- a growing number of top Indian managers are performing global roles based out of India, that is, senior talent staying inside the country. In early 2013, Yashwant Mahadik, HR Head for India at the Dutch company Philips became global HR Head, and chose to stay in Gurgaon for the role rather than relocate to Germany. Similar stories are seen in CapGemini, Cisco, Honeywell, Whirlpool and others. The reasons seem to be that the boards want people who understand this major emerging market and who add diversity to the company's leadership team, and do not think it matters where they are based as long as they are prepared to travel and stay connected.

- an increasing number of affluent and/or ambitious NRIs who grew up and were educated abroad are returning with young families. They live in the major cities and are bringing their expertise 'back' to India. They can afford a lifestyle rare in Western countries, but are also returning to grow new businesses based on middle-class Indians' ambitions to have Western-style products and services, and innovate for sustainability. An example is Dasra, a 'strategic philanthropy' organisation bringing high-net-worth individuals from India and Western countries together in philanthropic projects. Dasra was co-founded by the son of an Indian couple who emigrated to the USA in the 1960s and worked for Morgan Stanley before taking his expertise to India and using it specifically for social upliftment programmes. Another is Monitor Deloitte's Inclusive Markets, aiming to build a million affordable housing units where employees include a key employee born in India but brought up in Singapore, who then studied and lived in Denmark, Canada and the USA before returning to India.

It's not easy to do business in India. Policies are often out-dated, complex or ignored; bureaucracy is high, infrastructure and energy supplies are poor, permits are slow. Delays in all aspects of business are common, and corruption is pervasive. In the World Bank's 2013 Ease of Doing Business report, India ranked 132nd globally, below Brazil, China and Russia. The same report shows that starting a new business, sourcing electricity, protecting investors and resolving insolvency are all getting harder.

Just as it's not easy to do business in India, it's not easy to run sustainability projects. However, many international businesses are trying, and bringing with them central policies or ambitions on sustainability.

Big business and SMEs

India is home to some of the largest and most diverse conglomerates in the world, as well as the largest number of small and medium-sized enterprises (SMEs). The large group companies provide telecommunications, power, infrastructure, electronics, minerals, clothes and more, and the SMEs provide textiles, leather and agricultural crops; polish diamonds; repair things; run food stalls; and drive and more. Textile manufacturing is the second largest source of employment (over 20 million people) after agriculture and accounts for 20% of manufacturing output. Seventy-five to eighty percent of businesses are family-run, and Business Today estimates that these businesses account for 25% of India's sales and 32% of profits after tax. India's retail sector is the fastest growing in the world, estimated at $450 billion and expected to reach $637 billion by 2015. Different areas have varied business profiles – Bangalore's IT and communications expertise is known globally, Gujarat and the Punjab are entrepreneurial and internationally focused, Kolkata is home to several big business headquarters, and Mumbai known as a finance centre and the home of the majority of big business headquarters.

> *Indian industry is varied – it's important to know the key targets for your sustainability engagement, and tailor your programme accordingly.*

Investing and partnering

Some other factors to consider are the regulations around Foreign Direct Investment and whether your company is able to operate in India without input from a national company, as well as the huge value of partnering with an Indian company out of choice (one of several obvious benefits being the already-recognised brand). Maruti Suzuki is one of India's most successful car manufacturers. They are popular for many reasons, for example, it's easy to find parts across the country, there's a broad range of vehicles on offer, etc., but also because consumers feel they are buying a vehicle which combines the technological expertise of a Japanese car manufacturer (Suzuki) with the home-grown understanding of what an Indian needs from a car (Maruti). In the eyes of the potential customer, it brings the best of both worlds.

> *Partnering for sustainability, just as companies partner for business, can be the most successful way to go.*

Starting out

There are varied and excellent books on how to do business in India, and this publication doesn't attempt to duplicate them. However, any serious reader would find it valuable to dip into a few to understand the terrain you'll be navigating: see chapter 8 for some recommendations and why.

There are a growing number of service companies that help international businesses navigate the complexities of setting up an office or project venture in the country. The support of these companies is invaluable, but their input must be combined with putting someone 'on the ground' to do the background and help your company really understand its scope for work in India. That person can be a local person who knows India well but less so the company, or someone from the company who doesn't yet know India – or the perfect combination of someone who knows both. It is resource-intensive and a long period of time should be expected (at least 18 months) to really understand if expanding is valuable, but it's essential to build these foundations well. From there, you can work with a service provider based in India to better understand what sort of office you might want to set up with which tax, financial, legal, visa, staff, etc. implications, and if appropriate, apply for recognition from the Government of India.

You may be considered an expert with valuable information because you're bringing sustainability expertise from abroad to India, but you are also learning about how to do business and operate there – seek help from qualified service providers who can support you.

Speaking and listening

Although the resources in chapter 8 will help much more, here are some basic points to remember during your first interactions or visits, and their relevance to sustainability.

....

TABLE 2. First interaction points to remember

Headline characteristic	Detail of characteristic in India	Relevance to a sustainability project in India
Saying 'no'	In any situation, being able to preserve harmony, 'save face' and avoid saying 'no' is crucial to an Indian. Although it can be hugely frustrating to have a question answered 'yes' then to find out later that it's false, you must realise that if the Indian knows you are expecting one kind of answer, giving you that answer is a face-saving measure that comes naturally. This need to preserve harmony (and therefore continue the harmony of the group) is explained well in Craig Storti's book, chapter two. It can cause the most frustration for foreigners working with or in an Indian environment, and is vital to try to understand.	In many new sustainability-related projects, delays occur as new systems are put in place and because behaviour change takes time. Ensure you really do understand the ongoing status of your project by allowing Indian implementers to inform you about delays or challenges without feeling like they are letting you down or not meeting your expectations. Even within a trusted relationship built up over time, listen for the unspoken words which warn of a hitch in a project, not just the response you were hoping to hear.

....

Headline characteristic	Detail of characteristic in India	Relevance to a sustainability project in India
English isn't the same language the world over, but it is the language of international business in India	Just because many Indian business people speak English, it doesn't mean it's identical to what you hear in the UK or USA. I learnt the hard way that the phrase often used in England 'It's a shame' – e.g. 'It's a shame you cannot make the conference but no problem . . .' – will be read by an Indian as 'You are bringing shame on yourself and your company' (by not attending the conference). It's deeply offensive and considered very judgmental as only that person fully knows the reason they are not attending, not you. In an international context this offence might be overlooked, but don't just presume the same words have the same meaning. Although nearly all business people you will encounter will speak English, as well as at least one of the country's 200+ languages, using English represents authority,	Speak English in formal business meetings to show respect, however, don't presume you will follow all the meeting's English and do ask for clarification if needed. If English is not your mother tongue you may struggle with the speed of Indian speech – again, ask for clarification where needed. Make the effort to learn a very basic level of the local language if you are working with communities – it will cause much amusement but also break down some barriers and build trust. Knowing a bit about the language spoken other than English can be helpful, too. For example, Hindi doesn't use superfluous words – there is no word for 'please', no demonstration of gratitude as in Western countries because something is often done as a duty not as a favour: 'give me that dish', 'move here'. English spoken like

Headline characteristic	Detail of characteristic in India	Relevance to a sustainability project in India
	education and status. Therefore even if you're learning some, e.g., Hindi, it wouldn't be appropriate to use it in formal business environments – it would imply that you don't think the person you're dealing with is educated enough to speak good English. By all means if you build a relationship with someone over time, let them know you're learning, and they will endlessly be entertained by your efforts, but stick to English when doing business.	this isn't rude, it's just an end result of using another language more. As in all sustainability practice, use the words which mean the most to your audience, e.g. in rural India talk about meeting basic needs; with government, talk about poverty alleviation; with business colleagues, talk about the links to business growth and competitiveness.
Illiteracy	Many lower level workers or rural community inhabitants cannot read or write	Often written manuals or behaviour change documents will not be successful – appropriate communication methods must be found. For example, see Hindustan Unilever's 'roti reminder' at the Kumbh Mela in 2013. During the mela, HUL staff used a heated stamp to burn a Hindi language message about hand-washing into 2 million rotis (bread)

Headline characteristic	Detail of characteristic in India	Relevance to a sustainability project in India
Formality and dress	The business environment is more formal than in Europe or the USA (not so for Japan), and it's good etiquette to refer to people you are meeting as Sir or Madam, probably later changing to Mr or Miss, then the first name. In a business environment, it's customary to shake hands in greeting, but if meeting communities or individuals, it would be more appropriate to hold your hands together in front of your chest in a 'namaste' greeting.	Be respectful and a little more formal than in Europe or the USA especially at the start of relationships. If you meet villagers in small communities, you will be considered as an honoured guest and should gracefully accept all the welcome or food you are given. Due to the high temperatures most of the year, ties and jackets are rarely worn, however, it's generally expected that a foreigner would wear these to show respect. Very few Indian women wear skirts to work. If visiting communities, wear very practical clothes, e.g. you may well have to sit on the floor, walk on bad paths, etc.

Headline characteristic	Detail of characteristic in India	Relevance to a sustainability project in India
Religion and food	Virtually all Indians will follow various fasting days, prayer times or diets depending on their religion, and meeting times or food offered should be sensitive to this.	Follow the lead of those around you when eating and when in a religious building (you may well be taken to a temple if on a site visit – often CSR funds or charitable giving has paid for temples in rural communities), and ask questions about the religion – story-sharing is a passion.
The family unit	The Indian family unit is by far and away the most important institution to belong to – in a country where people cannot look to the state for health/financial support in a structured way, the family provides this system.	It would be seen as inappropriate not to respect someone's leave times (often at short notice) dictated by family requirements. Use the family unit to raise awareness on sustainability issues – mothers in particular will shape the behaviour of their families (Read more by googling Hindustan Unilever's story on *shakti ammas*).

Headline characteristic	Detail of characteristic in India	Relevance to a sustainability project in India
Hierarchies	Hierarchies are strong and highly respected in most business and social environments, so it's not always clear to see initiative taken (as only the senior person will speak).	Listen to the subtle voices in meetings – suggestions not elaborated on but ones which should be followed up individually. Follow the hierarchies the others make clear.
Making time for informal discussion	Informal discussion time, e.g. tea and lunch breaks in a working day, are important, to have individual conversations with people not willing to speak out in a formal and hierarchical group situations.	Always schedule several tea breaks into meetings, and/or finish a meeting with a meal or refreshments. This can be the most candid and effective time to speak with colleagues about the meeting discussion and their views on next steps. If visiting a rural community, use car journeys or evenings tours for more informal and private insights into the project and its challenges.

Headline characteristic	Detail of characteristic in India	Relevance to a sustainability project in India
Accepting meals or food	Business isn't conducted over food in the same way as abroad; however, food is nearly always offered to show honour to guests and to build relationships.	Do accept all offers of hospitality (I once had to leave a meeting I had thought would last an hour but took three followed by lunch to text someone I was therefore delaying. He responded back by text saying 'No issue Miss Caroline, Indian hospitality should not be declined').
Indian meetings	Meetings are slower in India, and should be viewed as the start of something, not the conclusion as often in Europe or the USA. Decisions are often not made during a meeting, instead views and results are shared and perspectives elaborated, and relationships built.	V Raghunathan writes: 'In India, more often than not we mistake talk for action, meetings taken for decisions made, reports written for action taken, speeches made for promises kept.' Do not hurry personal conversation, an important way to build trust and start a business relationship.

Headline characteristic	Detail of characteristic in India	Relevance to a sustainability project in India
Conference calls	Conference calls are hard because they don't offer the necessary breaks or enable body language to be read – make the effort to meet your key project personnel at the start and try to build this relationship even if eventually cemented over phone/internet.	Connections are often poor, people often take calls while being driven in busy traffic and English is spoken very fast, so lack of clarity makes international conference calls tricky. Don't try to persevere beyond the point of succeeding. Instead you have to make time to speak to all people individually, then organise a conference call to report back and keep all other lines muted.

Headline characteristic	Detail of characteristic in India	Relevance to a sustainability project in India
Meetings interrupted	In individual meetings with government officials, various documents will be brought in for signing, or others will join and leave the meeting as you speak.	Do not be distracted by comings and goings during your meeting time – take tea when offered, engage in small talk when asked, but try to get to the point of your visit fairly quickly if you can. As a foreigner speaking about environmental or developmental issues you will be seen as bringing an interesting external experience, but without a really strong understanding of the Indian context – do not be offended if you are told as such, it is probably true!
Corruption	Corruption is commonplace and processes are often built up around it; for example, 'ticketless travel insurers' in Mumbai enable people to take the train without a ticket, and, if fined, present their fee to the insurers who reimburse.	Ensure your business practices don't allow corruption and don't pay bribes as part of your processes. A sustainability-related project in particular should distance itself as far from corruption as possible.

CHAPTER 4

What You Need to Know from Indian History and Culture to Understand How Indians See Sustainability

IN 1972, THE INDIAN PRIME MINISTER of the day, Indira Gandhi, emphasised that removing poverty should be an integral part of the goal of the world's environmental strategy. In a statement full of foresight to challenges that remain today, she went on to explain that 'the concepts of interrelatedness, of a shared planet, of global citizenship, and of "spaceship earth" cannot be restricted to environmental issues alone. They apply equally to the shared and inter-linked responsibilities of environmental protection and human development.'

A father for the nation: Gandhi-ji

Such holistic thinking is based in the teachings of Mahatma Gandhi, the anti-violence leader of Indian nationalism in the 1930s and 1940s, and India's adored Bapu, the father of the nation. Gandhi's ethics included the pursuit of love, compassion, self-knowledge, duty and self-control, and he strongly promoted that all individuals should strive for *sarvodaya*, 'welfare for all'. As the economy grows and companies receive permission to oversee large-scale industrial growth, a conflict between Gandhi's philosophy and modern ambitions for national growth is often seen. Indian intellectual Rajni Bakshi explains that: 'In a place like India, people affected by large-scale industrial projects like mining are told that they must pay the price for the nation to progress . . . Gandhi fundamentally rejected this as immoral.' Another Gandhian philosophy was that technology was good to support people's toil, but not if it put people out of work, again a conflict with modern manufacturing industry. Gandhi also challenged the caste system and religious conflict (something very high in Independent India's memory following Hindu–Muslim violence during the Partition between Pakistan and India in 1947), and promoted the concept of trusteeship.

Trusteeship requires that we hold things in trust rather than own them for ourselves, giving a strong focus on a person's responsibility to care for the land or property or resource. Some key Indian industrialists have indeed applied the concept of trusteeship in their corporate responsibility efforts, and this shapes the structure of much of the country's corporate giving seen today.

....

Case study

Anyone who knows of Indian business knows of the Tata Group, and trusteeship is the model that best describes one of the early leader's view of himself and his role in the world. JRD Tata built the family business during his chairmanship 1938–1991, coming in direct contact with Gandhi during the Indian nationalist movement and chairing the company as the country wrote and implemented its first constitution as newly independent India. The Tata Group, now a $100 billion revenue business with around 450,000 global employees, has long been respected in India as helping to build the nation and caring for its growth and development. Although many business people in India and elsewhere do not often view Gandhi's approaches to be relevant to the modern-day economy, it's important to realise that many grassroots movements have Gandhian thinking at their core, and his approaches pervade aspects of all Indian cultures.

....

Gandhi's principles are embedded across many aspects of Indian culture, philosophy and business, and his approach of 'trusteeship' can be seen in varied situations in modern India.

An ever-present voice: Religion

Religion and spirituality pervade all aspects of Indian life, the business world included. India is a pluralist country with multiple religions and individuals are very much defined by their religion more strongly than in many Western countries. The majority of the population (80.5%) are Hindu – they live across India and believe in re-incarnation and so have a fatalistic faith in destiny. From a sustainability viewpoint this can lead to an inherent lack of engagement with long-term risks, for example, of climate change. Muslims comprise 13.4% of the population and follow key beliefs in the unity of mankind as one family, as well as fraternity and equality before a just God who rewards good deeds and punishes bad. The Qur'an says that human beings are trustees of the planet, and instructs them to look after the environment and not damage it. Christians make up 5% of the population, with majorities in Kerala and Goa in the south, and in the northeastern states including Mizoram and Nagaland. Christianity was formerly a higher caste/upper income religion but it now attracts Indians from all social backgrounds, often through access to education and missionary presence in the country and in poor areas. Christians take an ethical stance to business behaviour and apply that practically through philanthropy.

Sikhism focuses on egalitarianism and life in the real world: 1.9% of Indians are Sikh and many are known for entrepreneurship. With a very rigorous application of ethics, and a focus on non-violence and harmony, Jains are most present in Gujarat, Rajasthan and Uttar Pradesh in northern India. They are generally upper income people with a history of setting up charitable trusts and institutions including animal hospitals. They make up a small (0.4% of the population) but influential religious community. Another influential minority community is the Parsis (Zoroastrianism) (<0.1% of the population). These live almost solely in Mumbai and Gujarat, two key business states. The Parsi approach promotes morality, monotheism and enquiry, and its motto is: 'good thoughts, good words, good deeds'. Both the Tata and Godrej families, two of India's oldest and most respected group companies are Parsis. Finally, Buddhism makes up only 0.8% of the population, mostly in the northern and mountainous states. Regarding business ethics, the Buddha states that all employers should ensure non-exploitation, and provide employees with sufficient food, pay, medical treatment and support after retirement. In return, the employee is punctual, respectful and trustworthy.

Indians are identified by their religion to a greater extent than in the West, and the teachings of different religions can be seen in the way they approach philanthropy, charitable giving and modern corporate sustainability.

An embedded social structure: The caste system

The caste system, which originally organised the division of labour and power within Indian society, is often criticised for preventing social upliftment and maintaining inequalities across the country. Although there are examples of highly visible and successful individuals from the 'scheduled castes', the lowest castes, much more needs to be done to facilitate inclusion. It is a very political and sensitive issue, and the nuances are hard for a foreigner to understand, but discussion or action around caste can often be found in rural CSR programmes.

> *Much more effort is required to break down barriers created by the caste structure, some which can be provided by careful sustainability programmes which focus on equal treatment of different castes, social upliftment and capacity-building and skills development.*

An insight: Country-specific characteristics

India has a deep-seated cultural tradition to give to society and nurture the earth around. Yet there are glaring contradictions that need to be somehow understood in order that the policies and the emerging structures that support sustainable growth in India move in tandem with India's ancient culture and traditions. These are hard to understand without reading about Indians as a family unit. Fundamentally, Indians are family- and group-oriented, whereas Westerners are more individual- and self-oriented. In India the maintenance of the group, and harmony within it, is hugely important; however, it does not seem to extend to other groups or the collective 'we'. For example, individual homes will be beautifully maintained and carefully kept even with only minimum provisions, however, the area immediately outside the doorstep will be littered with rubbish and dirt – not the area of the individual, but of the collective and therefore not important. This can be hugely frustrating in a sustainability context, where shared resources must be jointly maintained and collective effort put forward by groups or communities wider than the immediate family unit.

The Ganges River is one of the five most polluted rivers in the world as it runs through the town of Varanasi. Yet 800 km upstream, Indian pilgrims walk for days to reach the sacred waters of Mother Ganges. They bathe in her holy waters, they collect her life-giving freshwater, and yet throw in their plastic waste and excretion just downstream: it's a collective resource and no-one looks after it. Some commentators have even suggested that game theory doesn't work in India, as people can lose focus on opportunities for collective improvement by becoming fixated on their own individual aims. For sustainability, and betterment of a communal space or resources, it can be hard to work with this characteristic.

....

CHAPTER 5

What You Should Know About Practising Sustainability in India

INDIA HAS BECOME A VERY SPECIFIC MARKET for sustainability, evolved along certain lines (see chapter 4). Recently, with the introduction of the Companies Act 2013 (see chapter 6), it has become highly government-directed, and is in danger of overly focusing on CSR spending rather than actual impact created. Sustainability has long meant efficiency in India – resource, time, labour and cost-efficiency. It has also long been seen as philanthropic, an obligation on a company to support the communities in which it operates, because that will lead the business to thrive. This philanthropy began to be described as CSR, which now often refers to social issues, with 'sustainability' bringing environmental concerns to people's minds. As with any country, a successful sustainability strategy needs to understand this context and the external expectations on the company, as well as consider the local political, institutional, environmental and cultural context. The section below aims to unpick some of this.

'CSR' or 'sustainability'?

This debate around wording is held in many countries globally, but it is increasingly accepted that 'CSR' has a philanthropic lean, whereas 'sustainability' is more related to core business strategy, risk and opportunity.

In India, this is slightly nuanced, with 'CSR' adopted to mean having a social focus and stemming from philanthropic actions of the past, whereas sustainability gives people an association with an environmental lean. Therefore a company often talks of its sustainability strategy alongside its CSR activities. In India there is a strong place for CSR, through which companies provide services that in other countries are provided by the state, for example, health or education.

Like the government, Indian business has generally been more focused on poverty alleviation than on environmental stewardship. This is changing as resource constraints become more apparent.

An inward-looking history . . .

India often turns away from international processes as having a key influence on its development. With an inherent and strong belief that international examples of anything from historical growth to consumer products are interesting but not completely relevant in the Indian context, it instead seeks to find its own solutions and pathways for its development. An example is that India is not one of the signatories of the OECD Guidelines for Multinational Enterprises (1976 updated in 2011 – India is not in the OECD yet other non-member countries have signed). These commit adhering governments to provide an open and transparent environment for international investment and to encourage the positive contribution multinationals can make to economic and social progress wherever they operate. Nor did the expert technical community adopt the internationally recognised LEED certification (Leadership in Energy and Environmental Design) from the US, but instead oversaw the development of an India-specific GRIHA (Green Rating for Integrated Habitat Assessment) designed to be more appropriate to the Indian climate. In international climate change negotiations, India has been seen as unhelpful at best and obstructive at worst as it seeks to focus on its own plans for carbon emissions reductions, rather than signing up to a global commitment it does not agree with. Long analysis on the intricacies of the above can be found and this isn't detailed here, but it's important to recognise that the administration is often not open to international commitments and instead forges its own processes even if operating on international issues or with an international impact.

. . . but gently growing international influences

As more and more Indian companies look to expand operations abroad, and as they join the supply chains of international industry, they seek to demonstrate they are capable of operating to international expectations or standards. Indian companies are increasingly joining global organisations like the World Business Council for Sustainable Development or the UN Global Compact, to understand and incorporate international voluntary practices into their operations in India and elsewhere. In addition, finance from donor governments is now focused on funding technical capacity and up-skilling, not traditional aid relief, and funds from international agencies like the International Finance Corporation (IFC) often come with social and environmental commitments. Indian companies also seek to understand and prepare for other countries' or regions' legislation, for example on emissions limits, which they believe will be adopted by the Government of India in time.

Philanthropy and CSR for poverty alleviation: Good news stories dominate

Traditionally in India, businesses took the approach that by contributing to the growing economy and providing jobs, they were supporting society and could exist in harmony with it. So CSR, originally philanthropy, has focused on education, health and religion, with very little, if any, integration into core business. Schools, health clinics and temples have been built in areas dominated by one large company, which must often also invest in local infrastructure for its own business operations as well as the wider community. There has been little focus on materiality assessment (a stakeholder engagement exercise to gather insight on the relative importance of specific environmental, social and governance issues to the business), and instead much focus on ad hoc charitable giving. In recent years, strong civil society groups have emerged and multiple media channels (particularly social media) rapidly spread stories of injustice or inequality. This has created stronger societal expectations from large companies, one of the drivers of why many bigger companies are now viewing sustainability more strategically and linking it closely to their core business. Hopefully, this will lead the way for broader uptake of this approach, and the National Voluntary Guidelines (p. 65) may help drive this further.

Poverty alleviation is often routed through support for SME growth. For SMEs, cost is king and improving efficiencies, thereby increasing the wages of some of the poorest people in India, is the first focus. If a cheaper alternative exists that's also more environmentally friendly than the original, that's fine, but it will be the cost that drives the final decision to implement. The SME sector is also very reactive: for example, if changes are made in one workshop, they will soon be seen in them all.

> *If needing to work with SMEs, find the apex body or association that represents that specific industry, e.g. SME Forum, SME Chamber of India, Small Industries Development Organisation (SIDO), Indian Industries Association, or state level bodies specific to industries of that area, e.g. the South Gujarat Chamber of Commerce.*

Risk or opportunity?

Although many companies state they perceive climate change as a risk, both because of future regulatory change and because of the physical situation, they actually see it more as a business opportunity. This is potentially because of involvement in UNFCCC's Clean Development Mechanism (CDM) projects. Water is increasingly seen as an operational and social risk. Poverty alleviation will remain the key focus and the language used for sustainability projects in the near future.

The availability and retention of employees is considered a huge risk to the sustainability of individual businesses and of India's economic growth as a whole. Companies have often developed their own training schools and capacity-building resources to impart the skills they need among their employees but which they don't believe are achievable in the education system (see chapter 7 for Infosys's example). Indian contract law makes it very hard to fire an employee, therefore much of the workforce is employed indirectly through contractors. It's much harder to have an influence over contractor behaviour than over a directly employed workforce, for example, around safety performance or child labour, and so this could prove a barrier in the implementation of widespread sustainability across Indian industry.

National legislation and frameworks: India's Five Year Plans

Since 1950, the Planning Commission has operated as an arm of the Government of India, chaired by the Prime Minister. It originally focused on developing Five Year Plans assessing the country's resources (material, capital, natural, human), and formulating a plan to use them most effectively for the nation's growth. Focuses were on issues such as agriculture, industrial growth, energy and irrigation, transport and communications. The Planning Commission of recent years is still charged with the country's Five Year Plans, but sees itself more as a vision-setter, helping the country and its leaders and citizens to understand the vision they should be aspiring towards, and urging them to implement it holistically. It aims to bring cohesion to policies that deal with integrated issues (e.g. water provision, poverty reduction), and has some of the most respected Indian thinkers among its membership.

The most recent Plan, the 12th (2012–2017) incorporates scenario-planning for the first time. Three scenarios are described under the headings Insufficient Action (or 'Muddling Along'), Policy Logjam ('Falling Apart'), and Strong, Inclusive Growth ('The Flotilla Advances'). A selection of Indians with diverse backgrounds developed these scenarios, and the National Council of Applied Economic Research (NCAER) was commissioned to create a macro-economic model that would provide quantitative rigor to them. Key areas are improving the quality of health and education to improve productivity; NCAER's analysis shows that a one rupee investment in human capital or in physical infrastructure generates a very similar growth impact. Three major policy levers are identified by the scenarios, and a document titled 'Scenarios, Shaping

India's Future' highlights some major initiatives which align with these:

1. Inclusion through livelihoods (generating employment or employability)

2. Governance (strengthening local, community-based and collaborative governance)

3. Sustainability (a 'green' lens to ensure energy-efficient and environment-friendly growth)

Read more here: http://planningcommission.gov.in/reports/ genrep/rep_sce2307.pdf

Look to the Planning Commission Five Year Plans for a vision for India, for proposals of holistic policies, and for the direction set by those with an ear of the country's leadership. These include specific visions for natural resource use, capacity-building and education, poverty alleviation and industrial growth.

Infrastructure

As discussed on page 23, infrastructure is severely lacking and poorly maintained, and energy can be erratic or cut off.

Poor infrastructure causes massive challenges when working on the ground in a sustainability project, the 'last mile' and rural communities being very hard to reach.

Environmental clearances

Obtaining environmental clearances can be a controversial and lengthy process. They are issued by the Ministry of Environment and Forests, which is reluctant to engage with businesses on broader sustainability issues for fear of being lobbied on individual permits.

Any company wanting to start operations in India should take into account the Ministry of Environment and Forest Environmental Impact Assessment (EIA) manual, requirements and technical guidance, categorised into 32 sectors: http://moef.nic.in/major-initiatives/environmental-clearances

Corporate governance

Not yet really considered within 'sustainability', corporate governance in India gained prominence during liberalisation in the early 1990s, as some private sector companies voluntarily adopted governance norms, led by technology companies. These companies were perceived to be well-governed and so were rewarded in the stock exchange. Fighting corruption is a core issue and companies are increasingly forthcoming in their commitment to anti-corruption principles. Corruption and poor governance is believed to be rife in government (it is estimated that nearly a quarter of the 543 elected members of parliament were charged with crimes of varying degrees in 2009), and business has an opportunity to build trust as governmental trust wanes. It is estimated that only 4% of the population pay tax, and only one in ten of India's workforce has a job in the formal sector, that is, with regular wages and hours.

Corruption can derail a sustainability project, or seriously delay a straightforward process. Be upfront about your company's policy on corruption at the start, and try to understand where there may be challenges in your project. Give colleagues at your headquarters reasonable expectations about timelines and be upfront if delays or blockages occur.

"Companies, in particular in the field of infrastructure, have to fight against corruption on a daily basis. It takes a lot of hard work, in collaboration with both external and internal stakeholders. What matters is to be committed to fight against it from day one and never give up, even if it means that the project might get delayed. It is also critical to create a culture of transparency that allows employees to discuss the issue openly. Finally, such a commitment has to come from the top management who needs to lead by example." BRUNE POIRSON, WORKS IN CSR FOR A LARGE FRENCH INFRASTRUCTURE COMPANY

Public Private Partnerships: Enthusiasm and confusion

In varied situations, PPPs are heralded as the answer to private sector input to societal needs, particularly around India's massive infrastructure requirements. Government officials state confidently that PPPs are the answer and urge industry to collaborate to build their cities. However, there is little clarity around different types of PPP, and what might or might not apply in different situations. The private sector is often viewed as purely an investor rather than being able to bring technical or process expertise and partners over the long term. It's important to clarify expectations and understanding when starting any discussion around PPPs.

Markets for sustainability: Growing consumer awareness?

Some optimists hopefully assert there's a growing awareness of sustainable products, of organic food and healthy snacks. Maybe this is true in trendy parts of Delhi, but there is not any large-scale demand for 'sustainable products' – except maybe where 'organic' signals no fertilisers have been used – because they're too expensive. In the construction sector, some corporates see the value in selling a Green Ideal, yet the messages are all quite confused: 'Eco!' claim the endless billboards lining the highways of major cities. New developments optimistically titled Orchid Island, Provence Estate or Nirvana Country rise out of the dry and dusty landscape and unrealistic drawings show the potential happiness that could come your way if you buy a flat in one of the shimmering new towers. Yet the reality doesn't look like the posters, with green lawns stretching out to clean rivers and clean public areas well-maintained for your peaceful arrival home from work. Here, 'Eco' means economical. And buying into it is another step up to eventual success and societal respect, despite the endless commute in unforgiving traffic and the electronic gates that denote the end of The World Outside and the beginning of My Home. In food and retail, some foreign brands are actually steering clear of trumpeting their green credentials in India so as not to confuse consumers in a new market without established trust in their brand.

A resilient place?

Sustainability is about being resilient. Indian people are resilient, but India's natural environment and its infrastructure are not. The vast sub-continent is hugely vulnerable to the impacts of climate change – melting Himalayan ice feeds the sprawling rivers in the north then churns southward irrigating the land; volatile monsoons lead to desperate droughts and withered crops; rising sea levels could gently slip into Mumbai streets and coastal industrial plants, and increasingly common extreme weather events pull political focus away from long-term planning and towards emergency responses every rainy season. Electricity blackouts are common and industry regularly shuts down due to lack of water for its operations.

A good document for more insight is GIZ's 'Sustainability Reporting: Practices and Trends in India 2012'. Because this outlines what and how companies report on sustainability strategy and action, it helps explain how Indian business views sustainability: http:// www.giz.de/en/downloads/giz-2012-sustainable-reporting-india-en.pdf

CHAPTER 6

What's Driving Business Action on Sustainability and What That Looks Like

A desire to build the nation

BUSINESS PEOPLE OFTEN TALK of the 'imperative of lifting millions out of poverty', here quoted from Azim Premji the Chairman of Wipro, and, as outlined in on page 52, large companies in India have long felt the responsibility to help grow India. This will remain strong in the future, and I expect there is a place for philanthropic and CSR programmes even alongside more strategic approaches to link sustainability action to core business.

Lack of access to raw materials

The Economics of Ecosystems and Biodiversity (TEEB) report estimates that 16% of India's GDP is directly dependent on ecosystems services, a figure that rises to 47% for the country's poor. It states that 350 million people in India are absolutely or heavily dependent on nature. Demographic pressures on natural ecosystems and communities with increased voices are making a social and environmental licence to operate harder to come by for Indian industry. Environmental clearances are lengthy and complex; there is discussion about extraction access being allowed in national parks in the near future because of limits to supply. Social opposition to resource extraction is increasing in many areas (the location of many mineral deposits is also the home of rural 'tribals' protected by law). Water is also increasingly scarce and operational shutdowns within industry are increasingly common.

International ambitions

With increasing numbers of Indian companies operating abroad, and foreign businesses looking to operate or sell in India, there's a feeling among Indian business leaders that it's wise to comply with international standards (on human rights, safety, emissions, etc.). This could help with access to foreign markets and funding. Indian companies are also looking to join international platforms like the UN Global Compact or WBCSD to support their understanding of global processes, regulation and best practice.

Changing policy environment in India

Some Indian corporate leaders believe that sustainability-related regulation or standards currently existing in Europe and the USA will eventually be adopted by the Government of India, albeit with some tweaking. Pre-empting these regulations will give the Indian company competitive advantage when or if those standards make their way to India.

In several sustainability-related areas, the central Government of India has good and progressive policies, yet translation to action at a state or local level, and accountability for that action, is often confused and incomplete. As we see more autonomy from India's states, some are developing their own standards or regulations to be seen as best practice and to support inward investment.

National legislation and frameworks: Companies Act 2013

In August 2013, the government passed the Companies Act 2013, which includes a new and additional driver for corporate sustainability action from within India: the '2% CSR spending'. The Act has overhauled and replaced the outdated 1956 Companies Act, aiming to remove legislative roadblocks to doing business, and therefore to India's economic development. It has a particular focus on strengthening corporate accountability, shareholder rights, governance and transparency, and is expected to prompt greater investment from foreign companies.

In a section unique to Indian legislation, the Act requires that every company over a certain size[2] spends at least 2% of its average net profit earned in the three immediately preceding years on social welfare programmes, or reports publically on why they have not done this. Strictly speaking the actual 2% spend is not mandatory as the Act requires only that a company reports on their CSR spending, saying they either have or haven't spent the 2% rather than actually holding them to account for the expenditure. However companies are putting strategies and plans in place as if it's a formal requirement. And if a company reports that is has spent less than 2%, it must explain why.

Key CSR requirements of the Act:

- Nominate a Corporate Social Responsibility Committee (of board members) and disclose the composition

- Ensure the Committee formulates a publically available CSR policy which outlines the company's CSR-related activities and recommends expenditure on each, totalling 2% of net profits

- Activities that can be included fall within nine broad areas (e.g. eradicating extreme hunger and poverty, promoting education, ensuring environmental sustainability) and should focus on the areas around that company's operations

- The Committee must monitor their implementation and progress, and report on them, or report on why the 2% has not been spent

Read the detail in chapter 9, section 135 of the Companies Act 2013: http://www.mca.gov.in/Ministry/pdf/CompaniesAct2013.pdf

Although the Companies Act has generally been welcomed, this particular provision has been controversial. Positives include the potential growth in CSR professionals and skills among the workforce, raising the bar by ensuring companies that currently have no focus on their impact now approach this in a structure way. Criticism includes a lack of clarity on what CSR means and which activities fall within the nine areas; a concern that some companies that currently spend *more than* 2% on CSR activities could, in fact, use the Act to decrease that amount in the future; that CSR becomes a 'tick box' exercise and not an integrated aspect of the company business plan; a lack of focus on understanding the *impact* of the expenditure not just the actual spending, or that innovation around long-term and collaborative projects that are having a positive social impact will be decreased. Mauritius has a mandatory

CSR bill with a clause requiring 2% spending on CSR, and Indonesia and Malaysia have also mandated CSR as part of company operations, but with India's size and business landscape there is much interest in its implementation and impact in coming years.

Note: as the Act was passed during drafting of this publication, updates and analysis are likely to be available online. Key things to watch for:

- Upcoming guidelines from the Ministry of Corporate Affairs clarifying questions around implementation of the Companies Act, and a list of activities falling within the nine broad areas

- A White Paper on demystifying taxation linkages of CSR activities

- Analysis of the impact of the Act on the social impact of business in the country, and positive and negative case studies of companies implementing the Act

- The first company reports that include reporting on this provision, and evidence from auditors that real impact is being assessed, not just spending

- Evidence that companies integrate this requirement into their core business strategy and not into philanthropic spending that doesn't relate to their business plan

❝The effectiveness of the CSR Clause 135 in the Companies Act 2013 lies in its implementation. We've given our inputs to the government on the rules to the Clause 135 that allows for creativity and innovation in social and environmental projects of companies. 2% is lot of money and if levered well, it can achieve a lot.❞ SACHI JOSHI, DIRECTOR, CII-ITC CENTRE OF EXCELLENCE FOR SUSTAINABLE DEVELOPMENT

National legislation and frameworks: Others

India's **National Action Plan on Climate Change (NAPCC) (2008)** outlines the country's voluntary mitigation actions to stem greenhouse gas emissions, submitted to the UNFCCC in 2008. It identifies eight core 'national missions' (e.g. Solar, Enhanced Energy Efficiency, Water, Sustaining the Himalayan Ecosystem). It directs ministries to submit detailed implementation plans to the Prime Minister's Council on Climate Change, and work towards those up to 2017, reporting along the way. It emphasises maintaining high economic growth alongside raising living standards in carrying out the missions. It clearly states that the missions will be more successful with support from developed countries. (**http://pmindia.gov.in/climate_change_english.pdf**)

Developed by the Ministry of Corporate Affairs, the **National Voluntary Guidelines on Social, Environmental and Economic Responsibilities of Business (2011)** contain nine 'principles and core elements' which aim to provide an 'Indian approach' to help companies work through corporate responsibility requirements and activities. They are compatible with globally acceptable guidelines on sustainability reporting. They stress implementation and are expected to be followed together, rather than allowing a company to cherry-pick activities. They cover, for example, community service, corporate governance, customer relationships, environment and supply chain management. The guidelines provide a framework to help companies create a holistic sustainability strategy and implement activities that fit with the 2% spending requirement of the Companies Act 2013. The NVGs also led to the Securities and Exchange Board of India (SEBI) mandating that the 100 largest listed entities must submit Business Responsibility

Reports as part of their annual reports. (www.mca.gov.in/Ministry/ latestnews/National_Voluntary_Guidelines_2011_12jul2011.pdf)

The Performance, Achieve, Trade (PAT) scheme is applicable to eight high energy consumption sectors which together account for over 50% of fossil fuel use in India. CO_2 emissions and energy use reduction targets are set for individual industrial units, in relation to the previous years' data, and energy saving certificates are awarded for exceeding target reductions. These can then be traded. The eight relevant sectors are aluminium, chlor-alkali, cement, fertiliser, iron and steel, pulp and paper, textile and thermal power, and the first cycle of the scheme is underway 2012–2015.

Sustainability reporting

India has a relatively low number of companies developing sustainability reports, and only a handful of Indian companies are listed on international indices such as DJSI and FTSE4Good. A GIZ report[3] from 2012 states that around 80 Indian companies from various sectors report at the moment, and about 60 companies publicly declare they follow Global Reporting Initiative (GRI) guidelines. Companies that already report on sustainability do so with a widely varying degree of clarity and content. They tend to focus on good news stories and CSR spending (in time and money), rather than outline how their activities relate to their core business and what is the quantified impact. In addition, an inherent distrust in voluntarily reported activities decreases the power that sustainability reports could have in India (helped in part by an increase in external third party verification as in other countries).

Various initiatives have increased sustainability reporting in India in recent years:

- Financial reporting already includes mandatory disclosure on environment and social matters, for example, energy consumption, raw material use and conservation efforts. Labour and industrial laws require reporting on matters including salaries, wages and benefits paid to employees.

- Since 2008, Standard & Poor's India ESG Index has required reporting on non-financial performance indicators and ranks 50 National Stock Exchange listed companies based on the environmental and social performance.

- The UK-headquartered Carbon Disclosure Project (CDP) encourages voluntary reporting of carbon emissions (and more recently, water use) by businesses around the world. It has been inviting Indian companies to respond to their questionnaire since 2006 (and seeing success) and has had a presence in India since 2010. CDP's 2012 report states that although the number of Indian companies reporting is not greatly increasing, the actual responses received are improving and the companies seem to be 'more confident' about disclosure. It also notes increased integration of climate change into business processes, and more transparency and better information around these.

- The number of UN Global Compact signatories from India has increased steadily and membership of the UNGC has been increasing.

- Emergent Ventures attributes increased reporting to international pressure and the desire to build a positive corporate brand.

The Companies Act 2013 is likely to change the style and content of sustainability reporting by Indian business; however, this won't happen quickly. As Indian companies respond to the Companies Act requirements, they will focus less on the international evolution of Integrated Reporting.[4] Although there is (some) Indian industry input to the development of the International Integrated Reporting Council (IIRC) framework, India is not likely to be a leader in this discussion, and is likely to have to focus its efforts on fulfilling national requirements before it looks to the new international framework.

When reporting, there is often a focus on amount of money spent, not on the impact of that expenditure. Donor agencies in particular are trying to drive change in this, for example, the International Finance Corporation work on baseline assessments and impact measurement in the sugar industry in rural India.

Any company starting a sustainability activity in India should look to deepen their own understanding of the impact of their actions by careful baseline assessments at the start of their involvement.

Awards, ratings and indices

Indians love awards, whatever they may be for. The good feeling created by publically appreciating an individual or organisation that has done well is the exact opposite from the bad feeling created when someone 'loses face' in a public situation. Visiting foreigners would be surprised to find house-sized billboards with names, photographs and exam results of the top school achievers posted in the streets. To incentivise action on varied fronts, the government at national, state and local levels, as well as other organisations and institutions, have a huge array of awards. Examples include the CII-ITC Sustainability Awards, the FICCI Water Awards, the

Golden Peacock Award, the Parivartan Sustainability Leadership Awards, the Saevus-Yes Bank Natural Capital Awards – the list goes on. Although some are no more than an excuse for a red carpet event, several, for example, the CII-ITC Awards, have extremely robust assessment processes, and provide detailed feedback to applicants to help them improve performance in future years. CDP reports include a CDP Leadership Index.

Similarly to awards, ratings and indices are popular in India. The Bombay Stock Exchange (BSE) recently launched the BSE-GREENEX index and BSE-CARBONEX indices which uses publically reported data to assess the 'carbon performance' of stocks and aims to create a market-based mechanism to promote energy efficient practices. It is hoped this will lead to increased investment in energy efficient businesses and provide incentives to measure and report non-financial data properly. In 2013 the CII Sohrabji Godrej Green Business Centre launched GreenCo ratings of manufacturing and services companies on various parameters including energy efficiency and water use (**www.greenco.in**).

There is a high risk that new and slightly different awards and rating indices continue to be issued by varied organisations, resulting in confusion and a lack of credibility for them all. However, unlike indices, awards are self-selected and, if you choose an award carefully, you can use it to motivate and incentivise Indian colleagues to take a structured approach to sustainability in their operations, to then report on it, and to gain recognition for success. At a very local level too, and at the start of a company's involvement in an area, awards or competitions can help engage local communities around your company's project.

Louder voices

As seen in the global press, there is an increasing disquiet stemming from the young and literate urban population on issues like corruption (see www.**ipaidabribe.com**), safety and pollution, and increasingly vocal opposition to government or business in rural areas where communities reliant on natural resources see access limited. There are also growing numbers of specialists in India working on corporate sustainability (p. 87 on) – industry associations such as the CII and FICCI have departments or Centres of Excellence focusing on these issues; research institutions such as TERI have business groups (TERI BCSD); NGOs such as WWF India are partnering with business, and in-house sustainability teams are growing.

Access to funding

Money is available to business to focus on sustainability to an extent not seen in the developed world. For example, the International Finance Corporation (IFC) has its largest operations in India, where it has invested over $8.3 billion in companies since 1956. It focuses its funding (including grants, credit, loans, blended finance) and technical expertise on resource efficiency, and on helping companies 'provide energy, water, roads, phones, healthcare, education, sanitation, waste management and access to financial services to people in low-income, rural and semi-rural parts of the country'.

On the other hand, national donors are increasingly providing funding to the private sector through technical expertise and capacity-building, a move away from the traditional aid-based giving approach.

Finance is also available from national or state governments. The Bureau of Energy Efficiency (BEE) (part of the Ministry of Power) has incentivised energy efficiency in eight of the most carbon intensive industries through the Perform, Achieve, Trade (PAT) scheme, effectively a carbon trading scheme. BEE also provides finance through funds, for example, the Venture Capital Fund for Energy Efficiency, or the Partial Risk Guarantee Fund.

❝After reviewing the programme and holding discussions with the Government of India this week, we agreed that now is the time to move to a relationship focusing on skills-sharing rather than aid.❞ JUSTINE GREENING, UK SECRETARY OF STATE FOR INTERNATIONAL DEVELOPMENT, NOVEMBER 2012

Returning Non-Resident Indians (NRIs)

An increasingly documented trend is the number of entrepreneurial foreign-educated or foreign-living Indians returning to the country with a stated aim to innovate and explore. Many left India in the early 1980s when there was little incentive for private sector growth, a number setting up in California (Indians are responsible for one in six of all Silicon Valley start-ups). For varied reasons, many are now returning. Their ambitions are big: 'widespread transformation' like Janaagraha aiming to increase citizen participation in urban local government, Hole-In-The-Wall e-learning from Sugata Mitra, or Kanav Kahol's Swasthya Slate Bluetooth medical indicator kit to improve health in rural India where the patient–doctor ratio is 20,000:1. Corporate India could look to tap into this trend to identify energised and professional entrepreneurs who are focusing on game-changing innovation.

CHAPTER 7

What Might be Coming Up in the Future

SOMEHOW THE POLICIES that support India in its urgent and spluttering lurch towards a sustainable future must mirror the practicalities faced by its governments, cities and communities. I can only wonder how well-conceived and inclusive policies can keep pace with the change India is seeing, yet they *must* be developed to provide a stable framework in which all businesses and communities can develop.

Conflict over land and natural resources

This is likely to grow and grow in the future as populations and industrial growth increases. Energy and water efficiency or self-generation will be a necessity for companies wanting to maintain their operations without shutdowns, and social tensions at a local level will increase without community-engagement and programmes of shared natural resource stewardship. Various products exist to help companies on their own path to efficiency and good resource management, for example, the Greenhouse Gas Protocol (**www.ghgprotocol.org**) or WBCSD's India Water Tool (**www.wbcsd.org/indiawatertool.aspx**).

Legislative change

The impact of the Companies Act 2013 (see above), and changes in Foreign Direct Investment rules are still to be seen. Increased FDI, particularly in the retail sector, provides an opportunity to set up stronger distribution networks, invest in infrastructure, and develop brands that reach rural communities and help all consumers choose products and services appropriately. It also provides an opportunity to bring unskilled rural labour into the workforce and integrate them in supply chains, helping bridge the rural–urban divide and integrating farmers and the rural unemployed into processing industries. However, the impact of changing rules in India and globally is yet to be seen.

Moving 'from patronage to partnership'

In the USA, strategies on deliberate supplier diversity have helped African Americans and women reach mainstream business opportunities. In India, Tata Group recently demonstrated a similar approach. Cyrus Mistry, Chairman of the $100 billion revenue Tata Group put one third of the equity into a joint venture with a little-known company owned by a dalit, entrepreneur (Chandan & Chandan Industries). They manufacture industrial safety helmets which will now be supplied to businesses across the Tata Group. The move to work in partnership with such a company was hailed as a historic moment in India, where hitherto charitable hand-outs have been seen as the only engagement with the dalit community.

The arrival of the commercial brand

Indian retail is still dominated by 'mom and pop' stores, that is, tiny shops stacked high with teetering boxes covering pretty much everything needed for everyday life. Produce is bought in a bag or newspaper directly from the store-owner who sends a skinny boy shimmying up a ladder to dislodge a box from the wobbly shelves then serves you from behind the till. Fruit and vegetables are bought from the market stall or a cart nearby. However, supermarkets are more and more common in large cities, and small supermarkets are springing up in rural states. They offer choice to the consumer, who is accustomed to selecting their choice of tea by volume of whatever brand is available that day, not by choice of manufacturer. In major cities, small supermarkets offer (hugely expensive) international brands, as well as local brands developed to sell packaged or processed traditional foods for the new consumer. Or there are small Indian supermarkets run by group companies offering a choice of products but not of brand. In some rural areas, these same shoppers can now step into an air conditioned-blasted, brightly lit room, with shelves offering everything from ready-mix dinner packets to tractors, alongside a room to measure the grain they're bringing in and selling to the supermarket owner to process or sell on. This is the model of ITC's Choupal Sagar (**www.itcportal.com/media-centre/press-reports-content.aspx?id=627&type=C&news=CHAUPAL-SAGAR-Unlocking-rural-markets**) shop outside Bhopal.

....

Food, drink and nutrients

As commercial brands develop, companies are likely to feel pressure to respond to social issues linked to their products. A key example of this is around food, drink and nutrients. Currently in India, consumption is king: 200 or so million middle-class people are suddenly accessing malls and shops. Brands are being developed and are trying to build up their own trusted consumer base. And retail regulation is changing to potentially enable international brands to have more direct involvement in supply chain management and operations.

Poor nutrition is affecting both the rich and poor – 'diabesity', the combination of diabetes and obesity, is a rapidly growing phenomenon especially among the young and in cities. Alongside this, the World Bank reports that the prevalence of underweight children in India is among the highest in the world with dire consequences for mobility, mortality, productivity and economic growth. A key factor in malnutrition is gender inequality, with women and girls often lacking sufficient and nutritious enough food. In many places there is poor education on feeding babies and children. Some companies are working to find solutions to this, for example, Hindustan Unilever's *shakti amma* scheme which recruits, trains, employs and therefore empowers women to distribute health and hygiene products to hard-to-reach rural areas. Dutch company DSM partners with the World Food Programme to fortify food and boost nutrition in the country.

Brand awareness is just developing, and an opportunity exists to build trust around international brands seen to be bringing foreign expertise or quality. There is very little marketing around sustainability in new products or services, instead the focus is on wealth generation or lifestyles. Some international brands are deliberately steering clear of championing their green credentials so as not to confuse customers in this new market where the brand is not established. Too much focus on sustainability can lead a consumer to feel they are being charged a premium for something where the benefit is not yet clear.

The challenge of effective waste collection, processing, recycling and disposal in India is huge. Very few formal systems exist, end markets for consumer waste are not established, and garbage is thrown anywhere and everywhere. Just a few years ago packaging was mostly biodegradable but with the introduction of plastic packaging, mostly by international companies, the waste challenge is huge and growing. Companies have a responsibility to help the country manage its waste challenge as their products are sold more broadly.

Tapping into Bollywood

Celebrity culture is growing in the country, fuelled by ever-expanding access to television and smartphones in even the most remote rural villages. A few Bollywood stars are promoting environmental or social causes, for example, actress Dia Mirza, who publically promotes environmental conservation and sits on the Coca Cola Foundation board; or actor Amir Khan, an active UNICEF Ambassador promoting childhood nutrition. NDTV Toyota runs an annual 'Greenathon' showing 24 hours of environmental coverage and urging donations from celebrities and high profile Indians. The world of celebrity is hugely influential, and increasingly vocal sustainability advocates from the red carpets of Bollywood could provide powerful brand ambassadors for corporate sustainability or positive causes.

A focus on skills

It is increasingly accepted that philanthropy and company CSR programmes are required to support the very poorest members of society, but the slightly less poor need skills and opportunities to help themselves move upwards. Companies are increasingly focusing on this in CSR, and in turn providing themselves with skilled labour. Mahindra Pride Schools provide vocational training to young people from disadvantaged communities. The three-month programmes have so far given a 100% placement record in the group companies. This was originally a CSR programme but has been so successful it is spinning off into a for-profit social enterprise.

In May 2013 French building materials company Lafarge launched a mason certificate programme to give young people job readiness skills and trade experience. Dr Camille M. Gonsalves, Country Head of Corporate Affairs and CSR at Lafarge India said: 'Our aim is to help potential masons develop the required skills and get appropriate job placements so that they can contribute to building better cities.'

Funding innovation and new ideas

Innovation in India is increasing: the President declared that 2010–2020 is the Decade of Innovation for the country and set up the National Innovation Council, but it is hard to upscale innovative start-ups. I heard many Indian business people ask 'Why wasn't the iPod invented in India? We have so many entrepreneurs, so much imagination, such amazing connectivity . . .' Companies have long given up on government funding for such research and development, and are now investing their own money. Through vehicles like P&G's Connect + Develop; Dell's Innovators' Credit Fund, or General Electric's Ventures, India Inc. spent $876 million on venture capital projects in 2012. For example, Omnivore Partners, a venture capital fund from Godrej Agrovet (the agri-business of the Godrej Group) has invested INR 240 crore/$45 million in start-ups on agricultural technology (e.g. weather forecasting, agric equipment, packaged meat) since 2010. Since 2011 Mahindra Rise has spent INR 2.5–3 crore/around $0.5 million funding the spread of new ideas across different sectors and creating a platform for entrepreneurs, in energy, transport and rural development. The Piramal Foundation, part of Piramal Enterprises, has spent INR 30 crore/$5.6 million since 2006 to back both not-for-profit and for-profit entities which have a social impact, for example, rural Business Process Outsourcing (BPO), or access to education or clean drinking water. As the Chairman, Ajay G. Piramal, has stated: 'If these models work we can take them to other parts of the world.' Could corporate India be a global testing ground for social upliftment through corporate funding of sustainability-related programmes?

Internal governance

The Carbon Disclosure Project (CDP)'s 2012 report states that 91% of companies responding to CDP India have assigned a senior level committee or executive body to develop a climate change strategy. A few Chief Sustainability Officer roles are starting to be seen in large Indian groups. As with many countries, responsibility for sustainability is creeping up the leadership levels in India.

An industry insight: India's IT industry

India's IT industry has been one of the great drivers of the country's recent rapid growth, mostly centred on Bangalore in the south. The industry currently accounts for about 7.5% of India's GDP and 20% of its exports. Several big companies vie for top position each year (e.g. HCL Technologies, Infosys, Tata Consultancy Services, Wipro), but it is Infosys which has become a symbol of India's status as 'back office to the world'. Having developed its IT business, it also now offers consultancy, helping understand and shape how IT can be used in other industries around the world.

The growth of the IT industry has provided millions of jobs for young people and offers global opportunities to the middle and lower-middle classes. Infosys has been in the midst of this. The company has long led a debate on improving the country's human resources, in particular skills and capacity-building among India's young population. Frustrated that graduate recruits were not trained adequately, it opened its own 'company university'. Infosys opened its $450 million, 350 acre Global Education Centre in Mysore outside Bangalore in 2005. It can accommodate up to 13,500 students at any one time, and is the first stop a graduate makes on leaving university to embark on a career at Infosys.

Using its expertise in technology, Infosys has also developed world-leading skills and systems in environmental efficiency and resource management, to make huge efficiency gains in heating, cooling, power supply, carbon, water use and money. It has an open manner which encourages sharing its experiences, at the same time as it is selling this technology and processes to companies around the world. This is helping to trumpet the argument that low-energy and low-carbon growth can profit a company and the country.

Another way Infosys has impacted sustainability issues in India is through a scheme conceived by one of its founders. Nandan Nikelani left Infosys in 2009 to chair the Unique Identification Authority of India, or 'Aadhar', meaning 'foundation' or 'support'. It will be the world's largest biometric database and will provide all Indians with a unique ID number to help access benefits and social care systems. It is voluntary and designed so people are incentivised to join it rather than forced, and, if it works smoothly and successfully, could change the current inefficient and corrupt way that funding, subsidies, healthcare or food entitlements are allocated to the poor in particular.

Developments in IT for the poor have also enabled access to energy, market information, food, money transfers and have supported business engagement with millions of people without traditional access to technology. Examples include ITC's e-choupal programme (www.inclusive-business.org/2012/05/itc-e-choupal-india.html).

Read more on how Information and Communication Technology can be an enabler for inclusive business in India and elsewhere: www.wbcsd.org/Pages/eNews/eNewsDetails.aspx?ID=14851&NoSearchContextKey=true

CHAPTER 8

What To Do Now

Your action checklist

THIS TABLE AIMS TO GIVE YOU some concrete next steps whatever the reasons you are reading this.

....

TABLE 3. Action checklist

WHO YOU ARE	WHAT YOU'RE AIMING TO DO	INITIAL STEPS RELATED TO SUSTAINABILITY	REMEMBER!
Senior management or leadership	Expand your business into India	Materiality assessment of potential operations in India, and assessment of how these are coped with by peers Put people on the ground to investigate partnerships and potential	Brand choice is only just developing in India. The opportunity to build brand trust is huge, but the risk of confusing consumers is also high

WHO YOU ARE	WHAT YOU'RE AIMING TO DO	INITIAL STEPS RELATED TO SUSTAINABILITY	REMEMBER!
Legal/ financial	Open up an office in India	Engage third party support company to provide guidance and manage the formalities with the Government of India	Bureaucracy is huge and timelines are often unaccountably long/delayed Choose a support company that's used to working with companies like yours (re sector/nationality)
Corporate operations director	Understand sustainability risks of Indian operations	Work out how your Indian operations will comply with new Companies Act Use tools like the Greenhouse Gas Protocol and India Water Tool to give top-line risk assessment	It can be hard to engage in discussions on future risks Funding is often available (e.g. from IFC) for operations improvements related to efficiencies/ emissions reductions

86

WHO YOU ARE	WHAT YOU'RE AIMING TO DO	INITIAL STEPS RELATED TO SUSTAINABILITY	REMEMBER!
Corporate HQ professional	Expand/ strengthen sustainability activity in your Indian operations	Understand the existing sustainability approach (including drivers) and action from your colleagues Visit an existing project in person to really understand the context and challenges if asking them to comply with HQ policy or targets Work out how your Indian operations will comply with new Companies Act	Timelines can be slow and it can be hard to obtain project updates remotely Local drivers for sustainability action might be different from HQ's, often because an understanding of sustainability is different

WHO YOU ARE	WHAT YOU'RE AIMING TO DO	INITIAL STEPS RELATED TO SUSTAINABILITY	REMEMBER!
Marketing or new business development team of international company	Launch new product/service with sustainability features or goals in India	Understand if your interpretation of sustainability within the product/service fits with the Indian market Work out how your Indian operations will comply with new Companies Act	Brand choice is only just developing in India. The opportunity to build brand trust is huge, but the risk of confusing consumers is also high Sustainability messages should always draw the link to increased wealth or improved lifestyle to resonate with the urban middle class or poor rural communities
Communications team of international company	Capture sustainability work being done by Indian colleagues	Visit in person to really understand the context and challenges Work out how your Indian operations will comply with new Companies Act	Challenge what you are told (may need to be done in person) as often only the good news comes through and real learning/challenges are not clear

WHO YOU ARE	WHAT YOU'RE AIMING TO DO	INITIAL STEPS RELATED TO SUSTAINABILITY	REMEMBER!
Commu-nications team of in-ternational company	Support Indian col-leagues in producing a national sustain-ability report/in-cluding non-finan-cial data in annual report	Understand the reporting context in India (p. 66) Work out how your Indian operations will comply with new Companies Act	Challenge what you are told (may need to be done in person) as often only the good news come through and real learning/challenges are not clear Different communi-cation is needed in India from an interna-tional audience It can be hard to get to the bottom of a 'business case' for community CSR projects
Supply chain manager	Imple-menting an HQ sup-ply chain policy in India	Visit to really under-stand the challenges Seek out international and country good practice	Corruption is system-ic, logistics are poor, contractor relation-ships are common
Company Foundation manager	Oversee projects in India	Partner with a credible Indian organisation and establish an on-the-ground presence/ team to manage this partnership	Long-term impact is more if work is in partnership with an Indian organisation An on-the-ground presence is a must

Your 'where to find out more' recommendations

The only way you'll really get your head round the complexities in India is to experience it for yourself. But as well, or instead, I suggest a look at:

- *Culture Shock India! A Survival Guide to Customs and Etiquette*, by Gitanjali Kolanad (Marshall Cavendish Editions, 2009): overview includes religions, economy, languages, natural areas, then focus on characteristics of Indians, fitting in as a newcomer, practicalities of living/operating there as individual, food and entertaining, language and communicating, and section on doing business. 'This book is meant to open doors, break down barriers, clear the way. India then remains for each reader to discover.'

- *Doing Business in India* (Ernst & Young, 2012): a guide aiming to help international companies understand the complex decision-making process involved in undertaking foreign operations. It outlines key industry sectors in India, recent developments in each of the sectors and the industry outlook: **www.ey.com/ Publication/vwLUAssets/DBI/$FILE/DBI_2012.pdf**

- *Doing Business 2013: Economy Profile India* (World Bank and International Finance Corporation, 2013): an annual report providing a country overview of business regulations in India, from the perspective of a small-scale entrepreneur. The processes involved in various business procedures are covered including dealing with construction permits, registering property, sourcing electricity, getting credit, trading across state boundaries and enforcing contracts. More analysis than practical guide, but important potential challenges are clearly outlined.

www.doingbusiness.org/~/media/giawb/doing%20business/
documents/profiles/country/IND.pdf

- *Games Indians Play: Why We Are the Way We Are*, by V. Raghunathan (Portfolio Penguin, 2006): gives insight into how and why Indians have cultivated behaviours that are destructive to the fabric of the larger community, e.g. around public infrastructure. Includes extensive experiments, research around game theory, prisoners' dilemma. Why Indians score low on self-regulation – they always want to try to get ahead as individuals even at expense of community. Common advancement: traffic, communal spaces, rivers.

- *Indian Companies with Solutions the World Needs: Sustainability as a Driver for Innovation and Profit*, by Sachin Joshi et al. (WWF and CII CESD, 2008): an exploration of how companies can use sustainability for innovation and profit, including detailed case studies from the Indian business world which aim to offer 'a range of ideas: from incremental changes to more radical business-model innovations; and from those that offer quick implementation and a short payback period to longer-term ones'. An energising read, it includes a strong call to companies to focus on disruptive innovation and look beyond the first few 'easy wins' for sustainability, e.g. energy efficiency. www.sustainabledevelopment.in/pdf/whatwethink_ Indian_Companies_with_Solutions_that_the_World_Needs.pdf

- *Speaking of India: Bridging the Communication Gap When Working with Indians*, by Craig Storti (Intercultural Press, 2007): importance of understanding cultural contexts, family as institution, communication techniques for both and interpreting the other (West v. Indian) management style differences, meetings, working with virtual teams, business and social etiquette.

Also:

- varied **Confederation of Indian Industry (CII) publications** at: **www.cii.in/Publications.aspx**

- the **Forbes India podcast** is very informative and covers broad and current topics on business in India

- many international consultancies with India offices have useful reports and research papers available for download on their country websites

Your 'who to talk to now' recommendations

CDP (formerly Carbon Disclosure Project)

CDP, which has a presence in Delhi, is an international, not-for-profit organisation providing the global system for companies and cities to measure, disclose, manage and share vital environmental information. It works with many organisations such as WWF and CII CESD to request climate change information from India's 200 largest companies (by market capitalisation as listed on the Bombay Stock Exchange [BSE]). In 2012, BSE launched Carbonex, a carbon index based on CDP data. In the near future, CDP plans to request water use data along with other partners.

From CDP's website you can download reports on company disclosure and carbon emissions trends and analysis from 2007 to 2012, categorised into nine key sectors. The reports give a clear insight into changes in corporate perspective on climate change, emissions targets trends, and the focus of sector leaders. Download from CDP India webpage: **www.cdproject.net/ EN-US/WHATWEDO/Pages/India.aspx**. For more information visit www. cdp.net or follow on twitter @CDP

ACTION: find out if your company submits data to CDP and, if so, where it sits among your peers; review past reports on CDP website

Centre for Science and Environment (CSE)

Based in Delhi, CSE is a non-profit research, advocacy and communications organisation working to promote the urgency of sustainability challenges and propose solutions. The five key work areas are 'communication for awareness', 'research and advocacy', 'education and training', a printed and online knowledge resource centre, and pollution monitoring: **www. cseindia.org**

ACTION: go to for targeted research partnerships

Centre for Study of Science, Technology and Policy (CSTEP)

Based in Bangalore, CSTEP is a non-profit research organisation aiming to 'enrich the nation with technology-enabled policy options for equitable growth'. Its 50+ research team work on energy, infrastructure, materials and security studies, and is recognised as a Scientific and Industrial Research Organisation by the Ministry of Science and Technology. Funding is from domestic and international foundation grants, industry trusts and governments. One notable example of its work was involvement in the Planning Commission's 12th Five Year Plan (2012–2017), in which a selection of Indians with diverse backgrounds developed scenarios to start collaborative discussions between citizens and policy-makers (the first time scenario-planning has been incorporated in a Five Year Plan).

CSTEP worked with the Planning Commission to develop the conceptual scenarios into a 'more robust systems dynamic model': **www.cstep.in**

ACTION: go to for targeted technical research partnerships

Centre on Energy, Environment and Water (CEEW)

Headquartered in Delhi, CEEW is an internationally reputed policy research organisation, funded by grants, project fees and partnerships. In June 2013, the International Centre for Climate Governance ranked CEEW 15th globally and 1st in India, in its first ranking of climate-related think-tanks. Research areas include publication of a 584-page National Water Resources Framework Study for India's 12th Five Year Plan; India's first report on global governance submitted to the National Security Adviser; undertaking the first independent assessment of India's 22 gigawatt solar mission; facilitating the $125 million India–US Joint Clean Energy R&D Centre; publishing research on energy–trade–climate linkages (including on governing clean energy subsidies for Rio+20); and designing financial instruments for energy access for the World Bank. It aims to join up sustainability discussions holistically, for example, working on the food–energy–water–climate nexus and multi-stakeholder initiatives to target challenges of urban water management: **www.ceew.in**.

ACTION: go to for targeted research especially covering several topics or industries

Cognito

With offices in Gujarat and Mumbai, Cognito India works on 'sustainability' (reporting, strategy, partnership), 'knowledgeability' (multi-stakeholder events), and 'brandability' (brand consulting). Its website has valuable insight reports, for example, a short infographic report on the 2012/13 Budget 'through a sustainability lens', for example, outlining changes on duties and taxes on low and high carbon technologies. Cognito is a for-profit company: **www.cognitoindia.com**

ACTION: go to for reporting and strategic consultancy

Confederation of Indian Industry (CII) and its Centres of Excellence across India

The CII is one of two of India's main industry associations (alongside FICCI), representing industry on numerous issues. It runs 10 centres of excellence, each headquartered in a different location and sponsored and championed by a company or individual. CII is funded by its members (industry), but the centres draw their funding from specific work streams, for example, advisory services, training, event management, grants. The three most relevant centres include:

- ITC-CII Centre of Excellence for Sustainable Development, based in Delhi. Work includes policy engagement and advocacy, capacity-building courses, very robust and credible annual Sustainability Awards and Sustainability Summit, publications including the quarterly *Sustainability Tomorrow* and thought leadership on sustainable and inclusive innovation. See more detail at: **www.sustainabledevelopment.in**

  ACTION: go to for training opportunities, online publications and case studies, company applications to Sustainability Awards or participation in the annual summit

- CII-Sorabji Godrej Green Business Centre, based in a LEED Platinum-rated building in Hyderabad. The technical centre offers advisory services to industry on green buildings, energy efficiency, water management, environmental management, renewable energy, green business incubation and climate change activities. Technical publications on specific sectors, technologies and research areas can be downloaded or bought from the website: **www.greenbusinesscentre.com**

  ACTION: go to for technical research and consultancy support on energy efficiency, low-carbon technology, renewable energy, green buildings

- CII-Triveni Water Institute, to have offices in Delhi, Jaipur, Pune and Bangalore. The young institute takes a holistic approach to water management, bringing together government, industry and civil society to focus on water and waste water management in industrial, domestic, agricultural and environmental sectors: **www.cii.in/CII_Triveni_Water_Institute.aspx**

  ACTION: go to for research and advocacy around water issues

Emergent Ventures (EVI)

Headquartered in Gurgaon but with offices in the USA, Europe and Asia, EVI is a for-profit advisory and research company working to access funding mechanisms for low-carbon technology. EVI oversees carbon credit project registrations and transactions, manages a portfolio of over 150 million carbon credits, and provides technical services to renewable energy projects. Staff are entrepreneurs, technologists, economists, community development workers, researchers and managers: **www.emergent-ventures.com**

ACTION: go to for support with carbon trading and finance, and CDM projects

Federation of Indian Chambers of Commerce (FICCI)

Headquartered in Delhi with offices across the country, FICCI is one of two of India's main industry associations (alongside CII), representing industry on numerous issues. It runs an annual sustainability conference with business and government (**www.ficcisustainability.com**). Sector teams cover issues including environment and climate change, health, urban infrastructure, for example, the FICCI Water Mission runs the FICCI Water Awards, and carries out research, for example, 'Water Use in India Industry Survey' and sector profiles on water use and action.

Futurescape

Delhi-based for-profit consultancy with a work area titled 'Sustainability: A portfolio of services that encompasses sustainability and csr strategy, implementation, communication and reporting'. Its website includes insightful presentations and commentary on current debates and action around CSR and sustainability: **www.futurescape.in**

ACTION: go to for consultancy support and online resources

Institute of Industrial Productivity (IIP)

IIP does much work 'behind the scenes', working with individual companies or convening industry with government and regulators on varied issues including greening of supply chains, low-carbon manufacturing and cleaner industrial production: **www.iipnetwork.org/ our-work-india**

ACTION: go to for technical and practical support on efficiency improvements, and government and regulatory processes

Intellecap

Based in Bangalore, Intellecap aims to 'shape outcomes for social impact' through investment and intellectual plus financial capital. To date, the for-profit company has raised over $200 million in equity for growing businesses that impact the poor and connected 400 social enterprises with over 300 investors and 160 mentors. It does this through investment banking services (raising capital and providing corporate finance advice predominantly to young and growing enterprises), consulting services (strategic advice and implementation support), and research on six key sectors: financial services, clean energy, water and sanitation, agriculture and rural business, healthcare, and education and vocational training. The company has also incubated and invested in several Initiatives and Group Companies that address specific challenges and gaps around Bottom of the Pyramid investment: **www.intellecap.com**

ACTION: go to for investment opportunities

The Energy and Resources Institute (TERI)

Headquartered in Delhi, this 900+ employee policy and technical research institution has offices elsewhere in India and abroad, and focuses research on biotechnology, earth sciences, education for sustainability, industrial energy efficiency, renewable energy and water. TERI developed GRIHA, the Green Rating for Integrated Habitat Assessment, India's national rating system for green buildings similar to the USA's LEED. Each January/February it runs the Delhi Sustainable Development Summit (DSDS), a huge cross-sector panel discussion and networking event. It established TERI University in 1998, offering graduate to PhD study in sustainability, CSR and environmental fields: **www.teriin.org**

ACTION: go to for targeted research partnerships, or attend the annual DSDS

The Energy and Resources Institute Business Council for Sustainable Development (TERI-BCSD)

This membership organisation of around 100 Indian companies aims to mainstream sustainability in business practices. Companies are convened around issues including energy, climate change, business responsibility and transparency, sustainable habitat and water; partners on specific business-relevant research, and brings out white papers on relevant themes. TERI-BCSD runs capacity building courses on, for example, greenhouse gas emissions monitoring and reporting and the Global Reporting Initiative. It runs an annual programme for Chief Sustainability Officers, culminating in the Leadership Summit for Sustainable Development. Its website includes weekly news clips, quarterly magazine *EnCORE*, and downloadable research reports. TERI is a member of the Regional Network of the World Business Council for Sustainable Development: **http://bcsd.teri.res.in**

ACTION: find out whether your operations in India are a TERI-BCSD member company, go to for membership and participation in the Chief Sustainability Officers Forum and annual Leadership Summit, as well as other work programmes and online resources

UN Global Compact Network India

The non-profit India network of companies signed up to the worldwide UN Global Compact, aiming to provide a forum for Indian companies to exchange experiences, network and collaborate on CSR activities: **www. gcnindia.org/about_us.php?page_id=10**

ACTION: understand whether or not your company is a signatory to the UN Global Compact and if so make the link to the India network, go to for networking with peers and advocacy on sustainability issues

World Business Council for Sustainable Development (WBCSD)

With a head office in Geneva and India country office in Delhi, WBCSD convenes around 200 global companies on sustainability advocacy and practical action. The global website is a wealth of free resources on business and sustainability, including many practical guides/ methodologies developed by companies for companies. These include the Greenhouse Gas Protocol (**www.ghgprotocol.org**), India Water Tool (**www.wbcsd.org/indiawatertool.aspx**), and the Business Ecosystems Training for India (**www.wbcsd.org/bet.aspx**). WBCSD worked on urban infrastructure in Gujarat in 2012 and published this free report: **www. wbcsd.org/uiigujaratreport.aspx**. WBCSD has an India office and several active working groups on varied topics including the Cement Sustainability Initiative for the cement sector in India. **www.wbcsd.org**

ACTION: see if your company is a WBCSD member globally, and whether your colleagues in India should be linked to the Delhi office. Go to for practical tools on your operations' water risk in India, business ecosystems training material, cement sector insight, membership, and working group participation with peer-networking

Foreign government presence

Many countries have a bilateral presence in India, and many have an international development or aid department, as well as a trade office.

Many foreign governments are refocusing their funding from traditional aid donations to technical assistance and support. Therefore funding can be available for various programmes or initiatives that partner with or directly support industry in India making environmental or social efforts. Examples include the UK's Department for International Development (DfID), which has a large office (**www.gov.uk/government/priority/supporting-development-in-india**); Germany's GIZ, whose website has many insightful publications of research, case studies and its work on varied issues (**www.giz.de/en/worldwide/368.html**); the European Business Technology Centre (EBTC) (**www.ebtc.eu**), which helps foreign companies with sustainability-related technologies to expand in India; Switzerland's Agency for Development and Cooperation, SDC, which runs a programme in India; and US AID, which has programmes and grants for business partnerships around health, food security and agriculture, clean energy, forestry and water, and education. **www.usaid.gov/in/**

ACTION: review your own country's India presence and whether they have dedicated resources to support business on sustainable growth/ low-carbon technology/inclusive business, etc.

Other websites

India Water Portal: great resource and platform for water issues including free sign up to regular news by email: **www.indiawaterportal.org**

India CSR: active online platform focusing on business and CSR: **www. indiacsr.in**

Sustainability Outlook: comprehensive reporting on sustainability issues across the country in particular related to business and the economy. You can sign up to daily news updates by email: **www.sustainabilityoutlook.in**

Newspapers: for example, *Times of India* **http://timesofindia.indiatimes. com/topic/Sustainability-Initiatives**, *Hindustan Times, Economic Times*

....

Notes

1. What a waste: How India is throwing away the world's biggest economic opportunity. *The Economist*, 11 May 2013.

2. That is, with a net worth of INR 5 billion (~$82 million), or a turnover of INR 10 billion (~$165 million), or a net profit of INR 50 million (~$800,000) or more in any financial year.

3. GIZ, 2012. Sustainability Reporting: practices and trends in India 2012. **www.giz.de/en/downloads/giz-2012-sustainable-reporting-india-en.pdf**

4. Led by the International Integrated Reporting Council. **www.theiirc.org**

For Product Safety Concerns and Information please contact our EU
representative GPSR@taylorandfrancis.com
Taylor & Francis Verlag GmbH, Kaufingerstraße 24, 80331 München, Germany

www.ingramcontent.com/pod-product-compliance
Ingram Content Group UK Ltd.
Pitfield, Milton Keynes, MK11 3LW, UK
UKHW040928180425
457613UK00011B/299